CARING
ANIMALS

A CHAPTER BOOK

BY ROSANNA HANSEN

children's press ®

A Division of Scholastic Inc.
New York Toronto London Auckland Sydney
Mexico City New Delhi Hong Kong
Danbury, Connecticut

For Donald and Edward,
who have taught me much about the art of friendship

ACKNOWLEDGMENTS

The author would like to thank all those who generously gave
their time and knowledge to help with the research for this book. In particular, warm
thanks and best wishes go to Allen Parton of Clanfield, England; Canine Partners
of Hampshire, England; Dan Shaw of Ellsworth, Maine; Don and Janet Burleson of The
Guide Horse Foundation in Kittrell, North Carolina; George Boyle; Ann Stein and
Judi Zazula of Helping Hands in Boston, Massachusetts; Roxanne and Gilly
Walker of Guildford, England; and Dr. David Nathanson and Christina Collins of
Dolphin Human Therapy in Miami and Key Largo, Florida.

Library of Congress Cataloging-in-Publication Data

Hansen, Rosanna.
  Caring animals : a chapter book / by Rosanna Hansen.
      p. cm. – (True tales)
Includes bibliographical references and index.
  ISBN 0-516-22912-5 (lib. bdg.)   0-516-24603-8 (pbk.)
  1. Animals as aids for people with disabilities–Juvenile literature.
I. Title. II. Series.
  HV1569.6. H36 2003
  362.404'83–dc21
                                          2003003721

© 2003 Nancy Hall, Inc.
Published in 2003 by Children's Press
A Division of Scholastic Inc.
All rights reserved. Published simultaneously in Canada.
Printed in the United States of America.

1 2 3 4 5 6 7 8 9 10 R 12 11 10 09 08 07 06 05 04 03

CONTENTS

INTRODUCTION

In this book, you'll meet animals that are trained to help people. These **caring** animals might bark or squeak. They might trot, swim, or swing by their tail. They come in different shapes and sizes, but they have some things in common. They are all kind, caring friends to the people they help.

Suppose you needed some special help. Whom would you turn to? How about Endal the dog, Cuddles the horse, Gizmo the monkey, or Duke the dolphin?

Endal can load and unload a washing machine. Cuddles can guide you through a city subway. Gizmo can bring you a bottle of juice. Duke can take you for a swim and then kiss your cheek. Let's learn more about these caring animals and the special work they do.

CHAPTER ONE

ENDAL, THE SUPER DOG

Have you ever seen a dog shopping for food at the supermarket or getting money from a bank machine? Those are just two of the special jobs that Endal can do.

Endal is a yellow Labrador retriever trained to help people. He lives with his owner, Allen Parton, in the village of Clanfield, England.

Endal shops for food with Allen.

Endal unloads the washing machine.

Endal knows how to help Allen with more than 100 tasks.

In 1991, Allen was badly hurt in a car crash. He was partly **paralyzed** (PA-ruh-lized) and needs to use a wheelchair. He has problems speaking and can't remember things. Thanks to Endal's help, Allen can do things he wants to do.

When Allen wakes up, Endal helps him

get out of bed. Next, he helps Allen get dressed and have breakfast. During the day, Endal is always at his side, helping with chores. Endal even knows how to load and unload the washing machine.

When Allen and Endal go out, Endal wears a special blanket. The blanket tells people that Endal is an **assistance dog**. Some days Allen and Endal go to the supermarket. In the store, Endal picks up many things from the shelves and puts them in the basket. Then he pays for everything and gets the change. If they need more money, Endal

Endal uses a bank card.

knows how to help Allen get some from the bank machine. Endal can even slide the bank card in the slot all by himself!

Endal was trained by Canine Partners. This group is in Hampshire, England. They have trained many assistance dogs. After Endal's training, he went to live with Allen.

At the time, Allen was sad and worried about his problems. He didn't like to talk to people, not even his wife and children. "I defended myself from people by being horrible and rude—that way I could be left alone," said Allen.

Allen and Endal started their training together in 1998. They took a course to learn to work as a team. As they trained, Allen slowly began to feel more confident with Endal. During their months of hard work, Allen learned that he could trust Endal completely. Endal "taught me to love, laugh, and live again," Allen said.

Endal helps Allen board a train.

Allen and Endal sometimes use a special sign language. If Allen forgets the name of something he needs, he makes a sign for it instead. When Allen taps the top of his head, Endal gets his hat. If Allen touches his cheek, Endal will get his razor. When Allen rubs his hands together, Endal goes and finds his gloves.

Wherever Allen needs to go, Endal is his guide dog. "Endal helps me by stopping at every road crossing until it is safe to cross.

Allen and Endal play golf.

I often forget to look," said Allen.

Endal is also trained to help Allen in an emergency. If Allen gets sick or falls down, Endal knows to pull a blanket over him. Then Endal knows to bark and to push an emergency phone button for help.

Endal has received many honors for his work with Allen. In 2002, he was named "Coolest Canine" in a national contest run by *K9 Magazine.* Allen has become a **spokesperson** for Canine Partners and for assistance dogs. Allen and Endal have shown that an assistance dog can help its owner live a better life.

CHAPTER TWO

CUDDLES, THE GUIDE HORSE

"Look at that little horse. It's wearing shoes!" That's what people usually say when they first see Cuddles. Cuddles is a **miniature** (MIN-ee-uh-chur) horse. She has been trained to guide blind people. She knows how to guide her owner, Dan Shaw, wherever he needs to go. Cuddles wears little sneakers on her hooves to help her walk. The sneakers keep her from slipping

14

Cuddles helps Dan get around.

Cuddles helps Dan get off the escalator.

on a slippery floor or an **escalator** (ESS-kuh-lay-tur).

Cuddles lives with Dan and his wife in Ellsworth, Maine. Cuddles helps Dan with all his chores. She leads him to his roadside mailbox, through stores, and around the shopping mall. When Dan eats at a restaurant, Cuddles waits by his side. If Dan goes on a car trip, Cuddles goes with him.

She rides in the back of their van. Cuddles stays in the house with them. When she needs to use the bathroom, she goes to the door, crosses her legs, and **neighs** (NAYS).

Cuddles is only 24 inches (60 centimeters) tall, with a brown coat and light brown mane. She weighs 55 pounds (24 kilograms) and is fully grown. When she is working, Cuddles wears a special **harness**. The harness has a handle for Dan to hold.

**Don and Janet Burleson with
their miniature horses**

Cuddles also wears a special blanket. The blanket shows people that she is a working guide horse.

Cuddles was trained by Don and Janet Burleson on their farm in North Carolina. The Burlesons were the first people to think of using miniature horses as guides.

They got the idea from their pet miniature horse, Twinky. They noticed that Twinky was friendly and **patient** (PAY-shuhnt), like a guide dog. So they began training Twinky to be a guide animal. The training went well. The Burlesons began to train more tiny horses. Cuddles is the first guide horse to finish her training and go to work.

Before Dan and Cuddles could be a team, Dan needed some training, too. Dan spent a month learning all about horses.

Twinky

He studied their **grooming,** health, and the way horses think and act. He learned voice commands, too. Cuddles showed Dan the body language she uses to guide him.

Dan and Cuddles became special friends. Cuddles likes to rub her head under Dan's chin. She sees Dan as a member of her **herd**. When Cuddles wears her harness, she knows her job is to guide and protect Dan from any danger.

Cuddles guides Dan across busy streets, stopping to show him where to find the curb. She always places herself between Dan and any cars or trucks.

She knows to look out for low branches. She chooses elevators and escalators instead of stairs. She can even ride on the subway in a busy city!

Cuddles rubs her head under Dan's chin.

**Cuddles always wears her harness
when she is guiding Dan.**

Dan and Cuddles on the subway

In his training, Dan learned to trust Cuddles completely. At first, he found it hard to give the little horse complete control. Cuddles kept guiding Dan and kept him safe. Once, she used her body to push Dan out of the path of a bicycle.

Cuddles has even learned to **disobey** (diss-oh-BAY) Dan's command if necessary.

Cuddles wears a special sign.

She disobeys only if the command will put them in danger. This skill is called **"intelligent disobedience** (diss-uh-BEE-dee-uhnss)," and all guide animals need to learn it.

In the wild, horses have shown a natural talent to guide other horses. When one horse in a herd goes blind, a horse that can see will often guide the blind horse and watch out for it. Horses have also been known to guide a hurt rider to safety. So, Cuddles has a natural talent for her job! Dan thinks she's the best guide horse you could ever imagine.

CHAPTER THREE

MONKEY BUSINESS

When George Boyle wants to flip on a light switch, he asks his monkey, Gizmo, to do it for him. George was in a car accident. He was paralyzed. He can't move his arms or legs and has to use a special electric wheelchair. Gizmo acts as George's hands and feet. Gizmo has been trained to help George with many everyday tasks.

Gizmo and George

When George says, "Gizmo, change," the monkey changes George's water bottle and inserts a drinking tube. Gizmo can also turn the pages of a book, fetch a videotape, wipe George's forehead, and open the refrigerator (ri-FRIJ-uh-ray-tur).

Sometimes George uses a laser light to show Gizmo what to do. The laser is on a thin rod that George can hold in his mouth. When George shines the laser on a book, Gizmo knows to bring him that book. When George shines the laser on a light switch, Gizmo will climb up and flip on the light.

Young monkey with her caretaker

Gizmo is too little to help George with some jobs. So, George also has people who help him wash and dress.

Gizmo was given to George by a group called Helping Hands. This group trains monkeys in Boston, Massachusetts. A monkey is trained for about a year. Then it is matched with a **handicapped** (HAN-dee-kapd) person. The monkey gets special training in tasks that its new owner might need. It may learn to help its owner do computer work. It can even learn how to scratch an itch!

Capuchin monkeys are smart and friendly.

At the same time, the new owner learns to work with his or her monkey. As they work together, the two become friends and learn to trust each other. After Gizmo's training, she went to live with George in his Alabama home.

Gizmo is a **capuchin** (KAP-yuh-shuhn) **monkey**. These monkeys often live for 30 years or more. So, they can help their owners for a long time. They are known for their friendliness and quick fingers.

Once they have a home, the monkeys become good friends with their owners. As George says, "Gizmo understands me. When I need a hug, she's there to give it to me. You can't ask for more than that."

CHAPTER FOUR

DOLPHINS HELPING PEOPLE

Dolphins are amazing animals. These large sea creatures are friendly and smart. They often swim close to ships, leaping and jumping high in the air. Sometimes they follow a ship for hours. Sometimes they help fishermen by pushing fish into their nets.

Dolphins have even saved people from drowning. A few years ago, a woman was swimming near

Dolphins can be trained to play gently with children.

This trainer is working with a dolphin.

a Florida beach. Suddenly she was caught in a strong **current**. The current was pulling her out to sea. She had given up hope when a dolphin swam up to her. The dolphin pushed her right up on shore! There are many other true stories of dolphins saving people or guiding them to safety.

In the 1970s, Dr. David Nathanson found that dolphins can help people in other ways. His **research** offers new hope for people who are **disabled** (diss-AY-buhld). In one study, six boys who were slow learners were shown new words.

Dr. Nathanson

Joe Jacks, son of an Olympic gold medalist, has
Tourette's syndrome (tu-RETS SIN-drohm). He swims
with a trained dolphin as part of his treatment.

This dolphin is playing with a disabled girl in Russia (RUHSH-uh).

When the boys learned the words correctly, they got to swim with a dolphin. The boys learned up to ten times faster than they had before.

For many years, Dr. Nathanson and other scientists did more research. They studied people with mental and physical handicaps. In each study, the disabled people got better when they could touch or swim with a dolphin. The dolphins in the studies were trained to work with people.

Dr. Nathanson was glad to find that dolphins could help disabled people. He decided to set up a **therapy** center with dolphins. People with **disabilities** (diss-uh-BIL-uh-teez) could come to the center to get help. Dr. Nathanson named his center Dolphin Human Therapy. He built it in Key Largo, Florida.

Since 1989, people from 54 countries have come to Dr. Nathanson's center for help. Many of the patients at the center are children. Roxanne Walker is one of the children who comes to the center for therapy.

Roxanne can't move any part of her body easily. The **joints** in her bones are too hard and stiff. She is in a wheelchair and can't speak or feed herself. Roxanne is nine years old and lives in Guildford, England. She goes to a special school there.

Several years ago, Roxanne's parents heard about dolphin therapy and thought it

**Roxanne Walker with her family and
the team at Dolphin Human Therapy**

might help her. So Roxanne and her mother made the long trip from England to Florida. The dolphin therapy did help Roxanne. Now she comes to the center every year.

Each year, Roxanne works on different goals in her therapy. Last year, Roxanne's goal was to move one of her arms. Roxanne worked with her dolphin and trainer each day. At first, she could hardly lift her arm at all. Each day, she worked to lift her arm a little more. When she made **progress**, she got to touch her dolphin, Duke.

By the end of the therapy, Roxanne could lift her arm as high as her shoulder! She could even reach out and touch Duke all by herself. "When Roxanne was finally able to touch her dolphin herself, her face lit up with a huge smile. She loves being with the dolphins," said Mrs. Walker.

Roxanne with her therapists and Duke

Roxanne also worked on holding her head up straight. When she did hold her head up correctly, Duke would kiss her on her cheek.

Mrs. Walker thinks that Roxanne has been helped a lot by working with the dolphins. "After her therapy, Roxanne can move much more freely. It's wonderful for her," said Mrs. Walker.

Dr. Nathanson said, "We find that many disabled patients can be helped by dolphin therapy. And it's great to see them have the joy of touching or swimming with a dolphin."

GLOSSARY

assistance dog a dog trained to help people with jobs they can't do

capuchin (KAP-yuh-shuhn) **monkey** a monkey that comes from South America

caring looking after and seeing to someone's needs

current a part of a body of water that moves along in a path

disabilities (diss-uh-BIL-uh-teez) problems with your body or mind that stop you from doing what you want to do

disabled (diss-AY-buhld) not being able to do what you want to do because you are ill or injured in some way

disobey (diss-oh-BAY) to refuse to do what someone says

escalator (ESS-kuh-lay-tur) a moving staircase

grooming washing and brushing an animal's fur

handicapped (HAN-dee-kapd) having a disability of the body or mind

harness straps that are put around an animal

herd a group of animals that are the same kind

intelligent disobedience (diss-uh-BEE-dee-uhnss) a skill that guide animals learn; they disobey their owners when it is necessary

joint the place where two or more bones meet

miniature (MIN-ee-uh-chur) smaller than the usual size

neighs (NAYZ) the sounds a horse makes

paralyzed (PA-ruh-lized) not able to feel or move a part or parts of the body

patient (PAY-shuhnt) being able to wait without getting upset

progress the act of getting better

research (REE-surch) work that is done in order to learn facts about a subject

spokesperson someone who speaks for a company or organization

therapy (THEH-ruh-pee) treatment that helps a person who is not well get better

Tourette's syndrome (tu-RETS SIN-drohm) a disease that affects one's movements and speech

FIND OUT MORE

Endal, the Super Dog
www.petplanet.co.uk
This website has a news section with articles on Endal and
Allen Parton.

www.caninepartners.co.uk
Canine Partners for Independence's website has
information on their work with assistance dogs.

Cuddles, the Guide Horse
www.guidehorse.com
The website of the Guide Horse Foundation has
information on miniature horses and on their work
as guide animals.

Monkey Business
www.helpinghandsmonkeys.org
The website of Helping Hands has information on the
monkeys and their assistance work with disabled people.

Dolphins Helping People
www.dolphinhumantherapy.com
The website of this dolphin therapy center offers
information on dolphins and on therapy programs.

More Books to Read

The Miniature Horse by Gail LaBonte, Dillon Press, 1990

Miniature Horses by Dorothy Hinshaw Patent, Cobblehill
Books, Dutton, 1991

Is a Dolphin a Fish? by Melvin and Gilda Berger,
Scholastic, 2002

I Can Read About Whales and Dolphins by
J. I. Anderson, Troll, 1996

Dolphins by Michael Bright, DK Publishing, 2002

INDEX

PHOTO CREDITS

MEET THE AUTHOR

Rosanna Hansen has worked in children's publishing as a manager, editor, and author. Most recently, she was a publisher and editor in chief of *Weekly Reader,* supervising 17 classroom magazines as well as book publishing. Previously, she was group publisher of Reader's Digest Children's Books.

Hansen is the author of many informational books on nature and science topics. She has written many children's books, including several on animals. She is also a volunteer with the Good Dog Foundation, which trains therapy dogs.

She and her husband, Corwith, live in Tuckahoe, New York.